For Joy Backhouse, with gratitude ~ P.B.

The Moses Basket copyright © Frances Lincoln Limited 2003
Text copyright © Jenny Koralek 2003
Illustrations copyright © Pauline Baynes 2003

First published in Great Britain in 2003 by
Frances Lincoln Children's Books, 4 Torriano Mews
Torriano Avenue, London NW5 2RZ

www.franceslincoln.com

First paperback edition published in 2005

British Library Cataloguing in Publication Data available on request

ISBN 1-84507-030-5

Set in Minion

Printed in Singapore

1 3 5 7 9 8 6 4 2

THE MOSES BASKET

Jenny Koralek

✳

Illustrated by Pauline Baynes

FRANCES LINCOLN CHILDREN'S BOOKS

Now there arose up a new king over Egypt, which knew not Joseph … And he said unto his people, behold, the people of the children of Israel are more and mightier than we … And the Egyptians made the children of Israel to serve with rigour: And they made their lives bitter with hard bondage, in mortar, and in brick, and in all manner of service in the field …

And … she took for him an ark of bulrushes, and daubed it with slime and with pitch, and put the child therein; and she laid it in the flags by the river's brink …

And Miriam the prophetess … took a timbrel in her hand; and all the women went out after her with timbrels and with dances.

Exodus, chapter 1: 8-9, 13-14; 2:3; 15:20

Long, long ago in the land of Egypt, there were thousands
and thousands of Hebrew slaves.

Once they had been shepherds who roamed far and wide
beyond the great river Nile with their flocks. But the powerful Pharaoh
began to force them to build his temples, tombs, pyramids and palaces
with bricks made from straw and mud, and to drag huge stones across
the desert for pillars and walls.

They worked hard. If they stopped to rest, cruel overseers would
whip them back to work.

And now the Pharaoh had so many Hebrew slaves,
he began to fear that they might turn against him.

So he sent out a terrible command: every baby boy born to a Hebrew slave was to be thrown into the river.

But there was one mother who was determined
not to let her little son die.

"I will hide him on the river," she said. "That is the last place Pharaoh's soldiers will go looking for babies. I will weave him a cradle out of papyrus reeds and I will cover it with slime and pitch so that it will float like a boat …"

The baby's sister, Miriam, ran down to the river as the sun was setting, and cutting a huge bundle of reeds, staggered home with them as fast as she could.

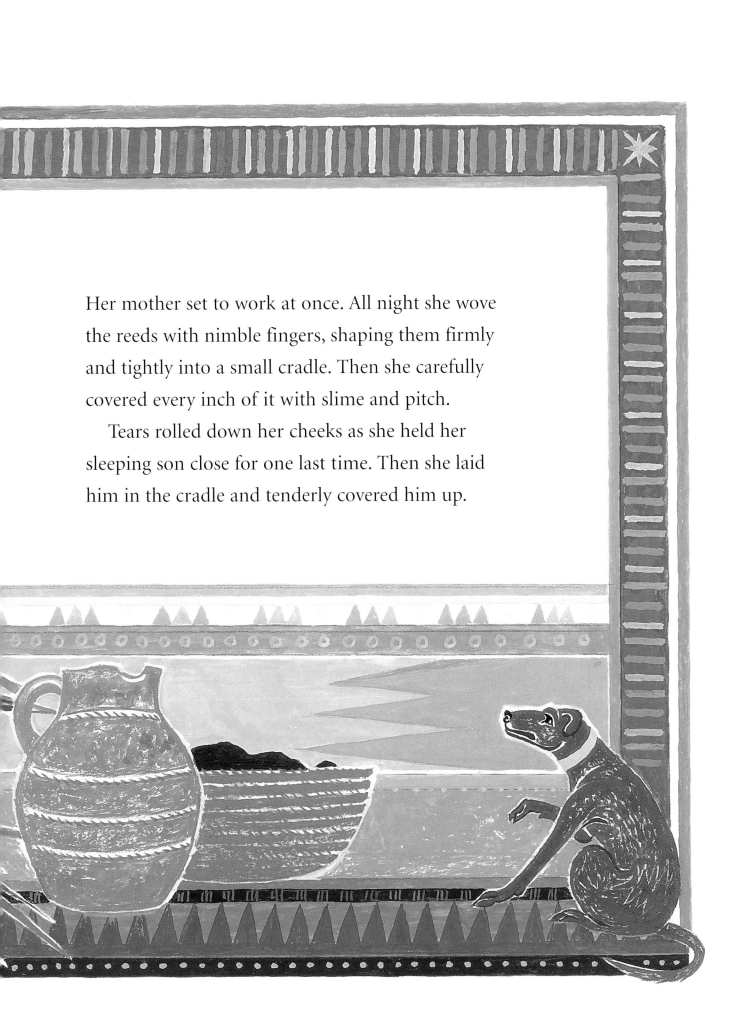

Her mother set to work at once. All night she wove the reeds with nimble fingers, shaping them firmly and tightly into a small cradle. Then she carefully covered every inch of it with slime and pitch.

Tears rolled down her cheeks as she held her sleeping son close for one last time. Then she laid him in the cradle and tenderly covered him up.

The sun was slowly rising, the great, burning African sun, as Miriam helped her mother carry the little basket down to the river. Their feet made no sound on the damp, sandy ground.

"Hurry, mother, hurry!" said Miriam. "She will be here soon."

"Who will be here soon?" said her mother.

"The princess! Pharaoh's daughter. I've often seen her bathing here early in the morning."

"If the princess finds our baby, she will kill him!" whispered Miriam's mother.

"No," said Miriam. "She will save him."

"How do you know?" said her mother.

"Because I know things," said Miriam, gently stroking the baby's head. "Remember how the house was filled with sunbeams and moonbeams when he was born? I knew then he was special … But quick, help me set the basket afloat."

Together mother and daughter waded into the shallow waters and gave the basket a gentle push. At once the basket began to float, like the beautifully-made small boat it was.

Creeping through the reeds, they followed the basket with the sleeping baby in it. Above them the sun slowly turned the river to gold.

And then everything happened at once.
A crowd of young girls, laughing and chattering,
came out of the palace and began running gaily
through the garden and down the steps.

"What did I tell you!" whispered Miriam.
"Here comes the princess! She's the tallest one!"
"She's seen the basket," said her mother softly.
"Look! She's sending a servant to fetch it!"

They hardly dared to look as the baby was laid in the princess's arms. He was crying.

"Isn't he beautiful?" the princess said. "He must be one of the Hebrew babies … Oh, poor little thing! He's hungry! He still needs his mother's milk…"

Then Miriam stepped bravely out of the reeds and went straight up to the princess. She fell to her knees and said, "Your Highness, shall I call one of the slave women to come and nurse the baby for you?"

The princess smiled at Miriam. She seemed to understand.

"Yes, child, go," she said.

Miriam ran back and fetched her mother, who came and knelt before the princess.

"I will pay you to feed the child until he is old enough to come back to me," said the princess, placing the baby in his mother's arms. "Then I shall raise him as my own son. He will be a prince, and I shall call him Moses, because it means *Drawn from the water*."

When they were safely home again, Miriam's mother
stared at her with tears of joy in her eyes.

"It all happened as you said it would!" she said.

"Yes," said Miriam.

And she picked up her drum and began to sing and dance, just as she would do many years later, when Moses led the Hebrew slaves out of Egypt into freedom in a land of milk and honey.

MORE TITLES FROM FRANCES LINCOLN CHILDREN'S BOOKS

The Coat of Many Colours

JENNY KORALEK

ILLUSTRATED BY PAULINE BAYNES

A long time ago in Israel,
ten brothers grew jealous of their father's favourite son, Joseph,
and of his wonderful coat of many colours. They decided to teach Joseph a lesson
he wouldn't forget... This exciting retelling, with images by one of the
20th century's most distinguished illustrators, makes
a perfect first Bible story.

ISBN 1-84507-053-4

I Believe

PAULINE BAYNES

Pauline Baynes, the much-loved illustrator
of C.S. Lewis's *The Chronicles of Narnia,* has transformed the Nicene Creed
into a joyous hymn to God. Her breathtaking images of the sun,
moon and stars, creatures great and small, death and resurrection are based
on a lifetime's passion for Anglo-Saxon and Persian manuscripts.
She brings them together here in a spirited affirmation
of faith to delight and inspire.

ISBN 0-7112-2120-0

Paradise

FIONA FRENCH

Twelve glorious tableaux portray the Old Testament
story of the creation – seven momentous days in which God created the world:
light and dark, sky and earth, fishes, birds, animals and finally man
and woman. Fiona French's images – inspired by the organic lines of Art Nouveau
and Louis Comfort Tiffany's stained glass – combine with words
taken from the Authorized King James version of the Bible to bring
the Book of Genesis into glowing perspective for readers
both young and old.

ISBN 1-84507-007-0

Frances Lincoln titles are available from all good bookshops.
You can also buy books and find out more about your favourite titles, authors and illustrators
on our website: www.franceslincoln.com